Miniature Pinscher Or Min Pin as Pets

The Ultimate Guide for Miniature Pinscher

Min Pin General Info, Purchasing, Care, Cost, Keeping, Health, Supplies, Food, Breeding and More Included!

By Lolly Brown

Foreword

Miniature Pinschers also referred to as the Min Pin, had become an increasingly popular dog companion because of its athletic, clever, fun yet poised personality. It is the kind of watchdog that has a huge personality wrapped up in a small and cute little package! And because it is one of the first ever dog breed that was recognized under the toy group, the Min Pins gained good reputation in the dog community and among dog enthusiasts which led it to gaining the title as the "King of Toys."

Find out more about this dog breed by delving deeper into its biological information. See if the Miniature Pinscher is the right companion for you and your family by gaining knowledge about its temperament and behavior, the cost it entails in keeping one, its health condition, its major pros and cons as well as how to feed them, groom them, and care for their overall well - being.

Table of Contents

Introduction

Despite the uncanny resemblance Miniature pinscher or commonly known as "Min Pins" are not miniature versions of the Doberman pinscher. In fact, the Min Pin arrived about a hundred years before the Doberman pinscher existed. You'll immediately recognize this lovely breed by its high stepping gait which is often compared to ponies. Most vets and owners think that they are like little athletes because they need lots of exercise, and lots of moving around. It might surprise you how playful this breed can be! Their very interactive and fun attitude as well as their fearless and proud projection is what makes them an interesting pet choice for many people.

This toy breed come in Red, Black & Rust, and Chocolate & Rust colors, and weighs around 5 to 10 pounds. These dogs are also known for their poise, and what many dog enthusiasts called "fearless animation" because they are tough little dogs. They have sometimes cropped but natural ears, and their tails are traditionally docked. These dogs also possess a compact and cat - like feet that allow them to walk efficiently, and with grace like a horse or pony.

The Miniature Pinscher's energy is perfect for training but it's only reserved for owners who are patient enough to teach them. Most pet owners agree that they are trainable but they need so much time and attention before they learn how to follow you. You need to be able to establish authority early on if you want to train them easily.

In terms of health, the Min Pins are generally a healthy breed. However, their small bones tend to be brittle which is why special care must be taken to ensure that these little dogs will have no problem in terms of mobility. While they are small and suitable to live in apartments, the Min Pin is a very active dog that needs adequate exercise; they are not lap dogs, so as a potential owner you have to prepare yourself on how to handle their active lifestyle.

Min Pins are also family pets but it's important that you socialize them at an early age especially if you have children so that they can get used to the idea of bonding with the whole family. Generally speaking, Min Pins can get along with anyone, even other dog breeds or household pets which make them a perfect companion! Find out more about this lively breed on the next pages, have fun!

Chapter One: Biological Information

    Miniature Pinschers are not just hyper and fun dogs, they're also clever, highly trainable, and served as a guard dogs for its keepers, but it may not be the right choice for everyone. In this chapter you will receive an introduction to the breed including some basic biological facts and physical characteristics, lifespan as well as the history of how it was developed through the years, and its roots. This chapter will give you background information about these pets, and introduce you their world! You can also find relevant information under the quick facts section of this chapter. Are you ready to meet the Min Pins? Read on!

Taxonomy, Origin and History

The Miniature Pinscher has a scientific name of *Canis lupus familiaries*. They belong in Kingdom *Animalia*, Phylum *Chordata*, Class *Mammalia*, Order *Carnivora*, Family *Canidae*, Genus *Canis* and Species *Canis lupus*.

This small breed descended from German Pinschers, and was developed in Europe about 200 years ago in Germany, though, several paintings and sculptures were found from the 17th century that portrays a dog similar to that of the Min Pins. It was originally named as Zwergpinscher which is translated as "Dwarf Biter" in German. Red – colored Min Pins were also referred to as "reh pinschers" by the German Kennel Club. Min Pins, like most dog breeds, are originally used for hunting small animals; they're pretty good in catching rats in farms and ranches back in the day.

Its body structure and temperament was inherited from their ancestors Italian Greyhound breed, and the Dachshund, but it's mostly the terrier blood combined with its Dachshund roots that drive these dog breed crazy making for some amusing, and fun moments at home or with the family. And because of their small yet regal bearing they're also known as the "King of Toys."

As briefly mentioned earlier, Min Pins are not a direct descendant of Doberman Pinschers nor are they mini versions of it. Min Pins already existed for over 100 years before Dobermans. In fact, Doberman Pinschers were bred and developed to look a lot like the Miniature Pinschers.

In 1925, Miniature Pinschers were officially registered in the American Kennel Club (AKC), and they are also the first ever dogs in the Terrier Group, but they became eventually classified as part of the Toy Group in 1930.

Today, apart from the AKC, Min Pins are also a member of several dog organizations all over the world including the Fédération Cynologique Internationale (FCI), Australian National Kennel Council (ANKC), Canadian Kennel Club (CKC), The Kennel Club (UK), United Kennel Club (UKC), and New Zealand Kennel Club (NZKC).

Size, Life Span, and Physical Appearance

Miniature Pinschers have a small, compact, and well – balanced body that weigh an average of 8 – 10 pounds for both male and female species. It stands at about 25 – 29 cm, and females have relatively longer bodies than males. Min Pins are generally healthy as long as you care for it properly; they usually live up to 12 – 15 years.

The Min Pin's body structure is square in proportion, sturdy, and also short – coupled. Its eyes are slightly oval in shape, and have a black or darkish eye color. Its ears are naturally erect but it can also be cropped sometimes. Its coat colors have three variations; a solid red color, black but with rusty – red markings, and Chocolate color with rusty – red markings as well.

Miniature Pinschers also have a relatively narrow head, quite long physique, and docked tail. They have short coats which make this dog breed the easiest to groom among the pinscher dogs, they're small which also means they require only a minimal expense in terms of grooming.

Quick Facts

Origin: Germany

Pedigree: descendants of Italian Greyhound; Dachshund dog breed

Breed Size: small, toy breed

Body Type and Appearance: Has a small, compact, and well – balanced body with proportionate legs, bright eyes, cropped ears, docked tail and tapering head.

Group: American Kennel Club (AKC), Fédération Cynologique Internationale (FCI), Australian National

Kennel Council (ANKC), Canadian Kennel Club (CKC), The Kennel Club (UK), United Kennel Club (UKC), and New Zealand Kennel Club (NZKC)

Height: 25 – 29 cm

Weight: average of 8 – 10 pounds

Coat Length: short and smooth coat

Coat Texture: smooth, soft, well - groomed

Color: Red, Black & Rust, and Chocolate & Rust colors

Temperament: energetic, fearless, friendly, sociable, and affectionate

Strangers: friendly around strangers

Other Dogs: generally good with other dog breeds if properly introduced, trained, and socialized

Other Pets: friendly with other pets in general, but if not properly introduce may result to potential aggression

Training: very trainable but requires patience and authority from their owners during training

Exercise Needs: highly needs adequate exercise everyday

Health Conditions: predisposed to common illnesses such as Heart Diseases, Dental Diseases, Arthritis, Obesity, Cancer, Hip Dysplasia, Lyme Disease, and Kennel Cough.

Lifespan: average 12 to 15 years or more

Chapter Two: Miniature Pinscher as Pets

After learning relevant background information about these fun and lively breed, it's now time to read the chapter that will ultimately lead you in determining if the cute Mini Pinscher is the right house pet for you. In this chapter, you will get a whole lot of information about the pros and cons of this breed, some legal requirements you need to follow before keeping one, how they deal with other pets, its personalities and behaviors, and what makes it a great pet. The primary things that your potential pet needs as well as the average costs for each items is also found in this chapter so that you can also be prepared financially. Keeping a dog is much like taking care of a newborn baby.

Is the Min Pin the Right Pet for You?

The main factor in determining if the Miniature Pinscher is the right pet for you is their personality. In this section you'll be given an overview of their behavioral characteristics or temperament, the cost of owning one as well as how you can socialize or introduce them to your other pets, and family members.

Temperament and Behavioral Characteristics

During the early times, the Miniature Pinschers are used to track down preys and hunt unwanted pests like rat farms. They have a natural instinct in preying on other creatures especially on open areas; this active behavior also means that the Min Pins are not the kind of dogs that should be left to its own devises.

As the years went by, they became increasingly popular as house pets. People have found a way to use their high energy levels and intelligence through proper training, and also by serving as a watchdog around the house.

These dogs are even – tempered and a very loving companion but its temperament is also hereditary. If you are seriously considering acquiring Min Pins as pets, one of the first things you can do is to visit the parents of the pups. You may need to actually interact with its mother to see how it responds to human touch or to people in general. Of course, you are looking for a friendly and engaging personality from the pup's mom but if that is not the case, you can expect its offspring (or your potential pups) to have the same behavioral characteristics and attitude towards people. There's a great chance that the puppies will reflect its mother's personality.

In general though, mini pins are alert dogs which are why it is recommended to train them or housebreak them at an early age, otherwise it'll be hard for you as the potential keeper to calm them down or discipline them. They don't usually enjoy repetitive trainings. If you want your breed to properly behave around other animals and children or other strangers, socialization and introduction is also a must.

Never leave these dogs unsupervised because they can become aggressive or wary to strangers. They are generally good with children but make sure that you teach them how to display correct pack leader skills, and always keep them in check. They are sometimes demanding and stubborn but they love to cuddle and have some play time with their owners.

Behavioral Characteristics with other Pets

This dog breed typically gets along with other pets but they are perhaps not the best dog to live alongside smaller animals like cats, rabbits, guinea pigs, rodents, birds etc. because of their natural instinct to chase and prey on smaller creatures which could cause injuries to your other household pets or to your dog as well. They will usually chase anything and disappear quickly if something catches their eye with no thoughts of its owner or its own safety.

They will get along with larger breeds of dogs but you still need to keep an eye on them because as with many toy breeds, they have a tendency to launch themselves at bigger dogs due to their fearless personality. That's how they compensate for being small in stature, which is not good if you are a pet owner because it could cause injuries to your dog or to other people's pets.

Pros and Cons of Min Pins

Pros

- Min Pins look a lot like an elegant Doberman Pinscher with a loyal, fearless, and fun personality that will surely make you enjoy their company.
- These dogs are short – coated which means that you won't have any problem in terms of grooming them, and can help you save on grooming expenses.
- Generally gets along with other dogs or pets as long as they are properly socialized and introduced.
- A lap dog and also makes a good watch dog; highly trainable, and an intelligent breed.
- A fun – loving family companion, these dogs are suitable for children and people in general as long as it is supervised and trained.
- Great pet for newbies

Cons

- Needs lots of exercise and a space to play with
- Tends to be a bit destructive when bored; must not be left alone at the house
- Can be extremely wary around strangers sometimes
- May be potentially aggressive to huge dogs, and can prey on smaller animals if not properly socialized.

- Naturally active and curious which sometimes can lead to trouble if not properly trained.
- Does not do well in isolation, demands lots of attention.
- Keeping them can be quite costly because supplies need to be bought all the time, and possible medical or vet expenses.
- Excessive barking and housebreaking difficulties; may need an authoritative trainer.

Legal Requirements and Dog Licensing

There are certain regulations and restrictions that should be taken in to consideration when purchasing a dog, or in this case a Miniature Pinscher. Acquiring a license for your pets can be different depending on the country, state and region that you are in.

In the United States, there is no federal requirement for getting a license for your pets, but it is the state that regulates these kinds of rules. Though it is not required for you dogs to get a license, it is important that you do so. It will not just provide a protection for your pet, but also to you as a pet owner. An identification number is placed in your dog licensed which is directly linked to your contact details as the owner. This can be very helpful in case your pet gets lost, it's also called micro-chipping.

It is also important to take note that before you can get your dog a license, you must be vaccinated against rabies. This is the only requirement for you to acquire a license. Dog license are renewable every year which means that you have to get another rabies vaccination.

Licensing for Dogs in U.S. and U.K.

In general, when you acquire a license for your dog you will be given a dog number that can then be linked to your contact information. If your dog gets lost and someone finds it, its license can be used to track you down so that they'll be able to return your pet to you. You can either use a dog tag (traditional ID collar) or have the option of micro – chipping your pet. Micro – chipping is a procedure in which vets will embed a chip on your dog's skin that contains contact details of the owner, and ultimately serves as a tracker for whoever will find your lost pet.

It is also recommended that your pet should acquire a license or be micro-chip even at an early age or while they are still puppies to be prepared if in case they leave the house without your supervision, during natural disasters, or if he/she accidentally access the doors, gates, or windows. This dog breed is smart and has a very short attention span, they can easily ran off if they see something that will caught their eye without you knowing.

If you want to apply for a dog license, you can search the website of your municipal or state government online. You will be able to download the application form, and just follow the procedure. After filling up the form, you can mail it to their office together with a fee. Although, in some states there is currently no fee for a dog license so make sure to check first and find out how much it cost.

Documentary requirements must be submitted before permanently getting a pet license such as current rabies certificate, spay and neuter proof, and microchip. In most states, these are the main documents needed to get a dog license, although, there might be additional requirements that need to be submitted in other states. The temporary license will be considered only as temporary until you have provided all the necessary requirements.

Travel License for Dogs

Licensing requirements for dogs is needed if you want to bring them along with you during your travels domestically or internationally. You may need to get a special permit if you plan to travel with your dog into or out of the country. In some countries, pets are subjected to a quarantine period to make sure that your dog isn't carrying a disease like rabies or other virus.

It's also recommended that you bring proper documents such as your state permit for your dog, rabies or vaccinations certificate, and a vet's approval or certificate that the dog or pet is in good health condition; to ensure that there'll be no transfer of virus or diseases to the country you wish to go to with your pet. Aside from that, there could be other requirements so be sure to check first the country laws regarding bringing of pets or travelling with them in other nations.

Cost of Owning a Dog

Most newbie dog owners ask experts how much does a dog cost. But the bottom line is that your potential dog will cost a lot more than just purchasing them because you need to feed them, groom them, buy accessories and toys for them, create an adequate environment, care for them when they're sick, acquire license or permits, and pretty much care for their overall well – being much like a newborn baby.

If you're not ready for a new set of "dog bills," then maybe it's not yet time to acquire a Min Pin or any dog breed for that matter. These costs will add up to your daily/monthly budget, it's really like adding a new member of the family. Aside from that, you also have to keep in mind that these pet expenses will go on for a long time since a dog's average lifespan is about 10 – 15 years. Not only that, when your dog dies one day, it will also cost you money.

To give you an overview of the major things you need to spend on for your Min Pin check out the following:

- **Purchase Price of Miniature Pinscher:** average puppy price is $500; if you purchase from backyard breeders you could bargain for it but make sure to check the dog's health quality. If you choose to adopt from a shelter, it may have additional fees of up to $170.
- **Food/Treats:** premium brands with essential nutrients can cost anywhere between $60 and $88 or more including treats.
- **Grooming Supplies/Toys/Cage/Other Accessories:** can have a total of $100 or more (depending on the brand/quantity).
- **Routine Vet Checkup:** around $260 per year; includes vaccinations, worm or tick preventions, and general routine checkup to prevent any potential disease that may harm your pet and cost more in the long run. It may also include micro-chipping your dog, spay/neuter procedures, initial blood test, and deworming.

- **Pet Insurance/Emergency Care Fund:** you should set aside around $2,000 to $4,000 to cover any unexpected emergencies, vaccination, medications etc.
- **Travel Care:** You may need to shell out $100 or more for kennel care if you're travelling a lot.

Chapter Three: Purchasing and Selecting a Healthy Breed

In this chapter you will be provided with the criteria on selecting a healthy Min Pin breed as well as a reputable and trustworthy breeder. You will also learn where to purchase a pinscher breed, and you can also check out the links provided in this chapter if you wanted to purchase a dog online or if you need information on where to visit a particular dog breeder. It's essential that before you purchase any dog for this matter, you should first consider on who takes care of them and how they are being taken care of, especially if they're still puppies. If you find a reputable breeder you can be sure to acquire a good dog breed.

How to Purchase a Miniature Pinscher Breed from Reputable Breeders

There are basically four ways where you can acquire or purchase a puppy:

- Private/Responsible Breeder
- Rescue/Adoption
- Backyard Breeder
- Pet Store

Pet Store

It's highly recommended that you stay away from pet stores. Most dog owners suggest not to purchase a puppy from your local pet shop because the majority of their available puppies came from puppy mills, and because good breeders do not sell to pet stores.

Puppy mill is a place where puppies or dogs are kept in solely for breeding purposes. It does not provide an adequate living environment, and dogs are mostly under terrible conditions. Puppies bred from puppy mills have lots of illnesses because of the poor environment. These puppies are then purchased by pet stores and sold to people. What most people don't know is where exactly this dogs come from, and how are they raised since birth. Many dog organizations and breeders advise the public or potential dog keepers to stop purchasing from pet stores so that these pet stores will stop buying from puppy mills, and hopefully force them to completely stop breeding puppies and raise them in horrible conditions.

Rescue or Adoption

Rescue is a noble thing to do but it may not be for everybody. Of course, if you are the kind of person who loves to rescue animals from shelter and raise them properly that's a great thing to do, but you have to be quite an expert or you should have previous experience in purchasing from rescue centers especially when it comes to selecting a healthy breed. You should also be aware of additional adoption fees as well as proper documents before you can officially claim your chosen dog.

The major advantage is that these dogs may already be pre-prepped already by its previous owners. Sometimes they already received all the vaccines they need, may have been spayed/neuter already, may have undergone micro-chipping procedure, and sometimes already trained.

However, you should still be careful when selecting from rescues especially in terms of the dog's health condition and/or behavior.

Backyard Breeders

Backyard breeders are people who breeds two dogs because they have purebred dogs or sometimes not purebred dogs, they breed them for the sole purpose of selling them or they just want to have a litter.

Good Breeder vs. Bad Breeder

Good breeders show their dogs or joins dog competitions

It doesn't mean though that they need to join on a regular basis because there are a lot of hobby breeders out there that shows there dog occasionally because showing is quite expensive. Nevertheless, they should've at least showed their dogs once or twice. The main reason for this is because it evaluates a breeder's breeding stock, and it makes them conform to the breed standard.

If the breeder has a showing experience it's quite a proof that he/she is following the official breed standard, trains the dogs, maintain their health conditions, and also provide them with the care they need to have a sound temperament and good attitude towards people. If a breeder is showing their dogs, it also means that they are breeding a high - standard quality of dogs. Bad breeders, on the other hand, don't show their dogs because they pretty much don't care at all.

Good breeders are valuable source of information

You're not looking for a smart breeder or someone who has a degree relating to animal care, but as a reputable breeder, they should know everything there is to know about their particular breed. It's highly recommended that before you purchase anything, you should be able to interview them, and make a list of all the questions you think is relevant and will be helpful to you once you acquired a puppy.

Good breeders are more than welcome to answer all of your questions, and are also open to discussing things thoroughly. You can ask about the dog's pedigree, their history, their health, how much to feed a puppy, the do's and don'ts etc. Good breeders should also be there for the lifetime of your dogs, and they should be able to attend to any questions or concerns as well as show some interest on how their dog is doing after you have made the purchase. Make sure to establish a good relationship with your chosen breeder because he/she will be essential in raising healthy pups/dogs. Bad breeders may not be open to answer questions, and even if they do, they may not answer it in an expert manner.

Good breeders know when to let go of their new puppies

A good breeder knows the proper age of when they can let their puppies go to other homes. It's a major sign if you're dealing with a good breeder or a bad breeder. Any good breeder knows that puppies should be kept until 12 weeks old, bad breeders will sell puppies under 12 weeks old. Bad breeders are only after the money, they are not concern with their dogs.

Good breeders will provide good references

You can tell if the breeder is reputable if he/she gives good references from their past puppy owners or customers they'll be willing to give it to you as compared to bad breeders who will not because you may discover how irresponsible they are based from their previous clients.

Good breeders know everything about their dog's ancestry

When you ask them regarding the puppy's ancestry, a good breeder knows things in terms of the health conditions of the puppy's parents, their size issues, the puppy's grandparents, temperament etc. Bad breeders have no idea how the puppies came about, where they come from, their background, ancestral health issues and the likes. You'll have a better chance in acquiring a healthy dog because good breeders know the health history or genetic problems that may have been passed down from one generation to another as compared to backyard breeders.

Good breeders only breed to improve their dog breed

Good breeders usually just have a couple of litters a year. Bad breeders on the other hand will breed dogs just because they have them or they're going to have tons of litters because they wanted to make more money. Good breeders won't breed their dogs until they are sexually matured (around 2 years old) while bad breeders don't care about their age, and will breed their dogs as soon as they come in heat.

Good breeders sell their puppies with contracts

Good breeders will only sell to people with a limited spay/neuter contract. If you're interviewing a breeder and they tell you that they're going to sell a puppy without a contract, you are best moving on because that's a huge red flag. Good breeders want to make sure that they protect the breed, and they don't just let anybody breed their dogs because they care so much about their breed, they wanted to make sure that their dogs will go to responsible keepers. A spay/neuter contract is done when selling a puppy to a new owner from a private/responsible/show breeder.

When it comes to contracts, good breeders also offer a health guarantee. Another thing is that before sealing the deal with their pets, good breeders will also ask questions about you, and your family, and what you are looking for in a dog. You can also show them photos of your home, or your family, where you work etc. though not a lot of reputable breeders require that. The important thing is that they're really concern about where their breeds are going to go, and it's not about the money. You should also be sort of a "qualified keeper" and pass their personal standards so that they'll have a peace of mind that these pups will be well taken care of.

Good breeders offers a reasonable price for their puppies

Bad breeders usually sell very cheap puppies, and it's because they never made any sort of investment in it. You can easily tell if the breeder is irresponsible if he/she is selling a dog for a bargain or way below the average price for a certain breed. Whereas good breeders will sell their puppies at reasonable prices (not too cheap, and not too expensive). Good breeders are okay with selling their puppies at a high – end price because they know that their breeds are of quality, generally healthy, and are well – taken care of. They made investments to their pets like showing them to meet the official breed standard, and various medical testing to ensure that their puppies are strong and healthy. There's obviously more money involve both for the reputable breeder and the potential keeper, but you can be sure of a healthy breed, and save tons of cash and headaches in the long run.

Avoid breeders who use words such as "teacup," "mini," "imperial" and the likes. It is not in the official breed standard, and the breeder may actually be just a backyard breeder enticing people with such words to sell their puppies or get rid of them!

List of Breeders and Rescue Websites

There are so many Min Pin breeders to choose from, that's why you need to do some research and decide which reputable breeder you should buy from before you start purchasing puppies. Here is the list of breeders and adoption rescue websites around U.S. and U.K.

United States Breeders and Rescue Websites

American Kennel Club

<http://marketplace.akc.org/puppies/miniature-pinscher>

Siggy's Paradise

 <http://siggysparadise.com/puppies-for-sale/miniature-pinscher-breeders/>

Mensonides Kennels

<http://mensonideskennels.com/>

Prancealot Miniature Pinschers

 <http://www.prancealot.com/index1.html>

Kruger Quarter Horses

<http://krugerquarterhorses.com/pups_for_sale.htm>

Puppy Spot

<https://www.puppyspot.com/breed/miniature-pinscher/>

Shadowmist

<http://www.bbtel.com/~shadow1/>

Puppy Find

<http://www.puppyfind.com/for_sale/?breed_id=139>

Min Pin Rescue

<http://www.minpinrescue.org/>

Animal Kingdom

<https://www.animalkingdomaz.com/en/miniature-pinscher/>

Pet Finder

<https://www.petfinder.com/dog-breeds/Miniature-Pinscher>

Woitas Acres

<https://www.woitasacres.com/>

Shiralea

<https://www.shiralea.com.au/pups-for-sale--min-pin-information>

Tea Cup Puppies Store

<http://www.teacuppuppiesstore.com/MiniaturePinscherPuppies.html>

Adopt a Pet

<http://www.adoptapet.com/s/adopt-a-miniature-pinscher>

True Heart Rescue

<http://www.trueheartrescue.org/>

Overstock

<https://pets.overstock.com/pets/Dog,Miniature-Pinscher,/species,breed,/?distance=25>

RescueMe

<http://miniaturepinscher.rescueme.org/>

MinPinerie

<https://minpinerie.ca/>

United Kingdom Breeders and Rescue Websites

The Kennel Club

<https://www.thekennelclub.org.uk/services/public/acbr/Default.aspx?breed=Miniature+Pinscher>

Pets 4 Homes UK

<https://www.pets4homes.co.uk/sale/dogs/miniature-pinscher/>

Champdogs UK

<http://www.champdogs.co.uk/breeds/miniature-pinscher/breeders?start=all>

Miniature Pinscher Club UK

<http://miniaturepinscherclub.co.uk/>

Preloved UK

<http://www.preloved.co.uk/classifieds/pets/dogs/for-sale/uk/miniature+pinscher>

Puppy Finder

<http://www.puppyfinder.org.uk/toys/miniature-pinscher/>

Chapter Four: Habitat Requirements for Miniature Pinscher

Assuming that you have already bought a Miniature Pinscher, it's now time to learn how to maintain them and set up a great environment for them so they can happily grow with you and your family. In this chapter you will learn the basics about your dog's habitat requirements including its shelter placement, housing needs. You will also learn some tips on how to dog - proof your house before your new pet arrives as well as some guidelines on how you can maintain an adequate living condition for them.

Ideal Habitat for Your Dog

Where to place the cage or play pen

Your dog's cage should be ideally place in the familiar part of the house. For toy breeds like the Miniature Pinscher, you can set up a cage or a confinement area near the living room or probably near the couch where you hang out often.

How to choose the right cage size

When it comes to choosing the right cage size for your dog, the rule of thumb is to purchase a cage that is twice as large as the current size of your pet. After which, it is ideal to also buy a play pen and attached it to the crate so that your dog will have his/her own space and also an ample area for feeding, playing, and pooping. Keep in mind to set the area away from direct sunlight or cold temperatures, and it should also not be set up directly under air cons and/or heaters.

Things are needed inside your dog's crate

When leaving a puppy for an extended period inside its cage set up, the crate should be the place where your dog will feel comfortable sleeping in, because it will help teach your puppy to be comfortable in his confinement area. Soft comfortable bedding should be placed inside your dog's crate. It's also ideal that you provide a blanket so your pet could burrow in whenever he/she feels like it. Min Pins love to be burrow in blankets most of the time. You might also want to provide your pet with its own snuggle puppy.

Toys for your pet

Snuggle puppies are a kind of plush toy with a realistic heartbeat and warming pet that simulates another puppy and helps in comforting younger puppies to transition from their breeder to being part of a family or as a household pet. You can also provide other dog toys (at least 4 to 6) to stimulate your Min Pin. Alternate the toys every week or every now and then, or find out what toy your pet prefers. It's also best to supply a variety of toys serve for different purposes to keep your puppy interested. Always supervise your pets while he/she is playing its toys. Here's a list of the kind of toys you can purchase for your dog:

- **Chewing toys** – it will satisfy your dog's instinct to chew, and also relieve pressurized gums.
- **Sense Stimulator toys** – you can buy toys that can stimulate your dog's senses such as toys that have variety of colors, sounds, or smells.
- **Rubber Squeaky Toys** – puppy's in particular loves to chew rubbery toys that make lots of noises.

- **Puzzle Toys** – serves as your puppy or dog's mental stimulation

How to set up a toilet space

When it comes to providing a toilet space for your puppies, you should make sure that the space is far away as possible from their crate or from where you are feeding them. As an example, if you have done some potty training already outside on the grass, and you want to train your pet to pee or poo inside its own play pen, you might want to consider buying a synthetic grass from your local hardware store. You might want to put the synthetic grass in a tray or buy a synthetic interlocking grass tiles. The synthetic interlocking grass tile is very ideal because it has drainage holes to prevent fluids from flowing; you just have to replace a puppy pee pad underneath it to soak up the excess fluids. Whenever you're cleaning the synthetic grass, you can just hose it down, and let it dry for a while. You can buy more than two square grasses so that you have a spare while you are drying the other set after cleaning it.

As a reminder, the toilet area inside the play pen should be located on the opposite side of your dog's sleeping area. However, the toileting sofa should be removed if you are at home, and should only be provided when you're away. The reason for this is that you want to avoid tolerating the puppy that it's okay to toilet indoors;

ensure that your pet poo or pee outdoors at every possible opportunity to accelerate toilet training.

Water and Food Dishes

You need to provide your dog with ample drinking water, and food bowls especially if you're going away for a certain period of time. Most owners recommend a non – breakable, non – spill water bowl otherwise your puppy or dog will spill its water, and will be left with no water for days while you are away.

You can also buy a ceramic or glass water/food bowls, however it is only ideal if you are at home because if in case the puppy breaks it, he/she might ingest the broken pieces or injure its food with the shattered glass. A stainless food and water dishes are also ideal because it's durable and also quite easy to clean. It's also safe for your pet, but it can be tipped over as well.

Housing Temperature

Another environmental factor you need to consider for your dogs is the temperature. The ambient temperature in your house should be at a normal range, not too hot and not too cold either. You should also avoid exposing your dog to too much sunlight because it might cause skin or coat issues.

Tips on How to Dog – Proof Your House

If you are still waiting for your pet to arrive, it's the perfect time to prepare your home (and yourself) so that your pup can be protected from various household hazards and be able to eliminate any unwanted accidents or situations. Below are some tips on how to dog – proof your house:

- Provide fences, a screened porch or a safe enclosure. Be sure to dog-proof your yard so that your dog could experience the outdoors safely.

- Remove any poisonous plants since dogs are naturally curious, and likes to chew anything. If your dog chew any plants, even the non-poisonous ones can cause vomiting and diarrhea or fatality.

- Install padded perches indoors near a window frame or in your patio so that your pet could enjoy and hang out but do not leave your doors and screens unlocked.

- Do not leave your appliances plugged, as mentioned

earlier, they will chew anything including electric wires, not only is this potentially fatal for your dog but also a dangerous threat for your home.

- Buy a harness and train your dog to walk on a leash when going around the neighborhood.

- Consider buying a ready-made dog tree to provide climbing opportunities for your dog inside.

- Make sure to keep lots of dog toys out and put anything precious and destructible away.

- Make sure to keep away toxic liquids or materials like cleaning supplies or other household items that can harm them.

- Make sure that your puppy will not be able to enter bathrooms or kitchens alone because it can be dangerous for them.

- Once your dog arrives, you can observe it as it explores and become familiar with your home, you'll and also get to discover some things you need to dog – proof.

Chapter Five: Nutrition and Feeding

In this chapter, you'll learn the majority of your pet's nutritional needs as well as some feeding guidelines, foods that are good and harmful for your dog. Proper nutrition will go a long way for your dog's health and growth. Feeding your Miniature Pinscher is not that complicated but you have to make sure that its level of activity, age, and weight should be taken into consideration to meet its nutritional diet needs. Min Pins should be given the right amount of recommended food for a balanced nutrition because proper diet can lengthen the life expectancy of your dog and also protect them from serious illnesses.

Nutritional Needs of Miniature Pinscher

According to most vets and dog experts, the best and healthiest diet is a home prepared, and well – formulated diet that contains fresh ingredients as well as canned, frozen, dehydrated and/or kibble foods. Most people feed their dogs kibble because it's very easy to prepare but many doctors and nutritionists suggest that even though kibble is the most common type of commercial food, your dog will still need a balanced diet from fresh ingredients.

If you are set in feeding your dog a dry food diet, and you are committed to buy the best possible quality food, you should first determine which one you should choose. One of the best ways is to try different foods, and see how your dog responds to each of them. It's also ideal that you keep a journal to note any changes that your dog indicates to each bag of food, or any signs of intolerance. It could also help you take note any signs of food allergies.

How to Select the Right Dog Food

It's best to purchase dog foods at small independent pet supply stores because supermarkets, groceries, superstores and the likes sometimes don't carry quality dog foods. After finding the right store for you, the next thing you should do is to look at the product label of the brand you chose, and examine its ingredients list. What you need to look out for are top – quality, and whole ingredients. It's not recommended that you buy foods containing proteins or fats from unknown or unnamed species (usually it is written in the ingredients list as "animal fat" or "animal protein"). You should buy whole ingredients that come from named or known species such as duck, lamb, beef, chicken, and the likes. Organ meats are by – products, so if a food contains organs of top – quality, it should be added in the ingredients list and named separately; an example is beef heart and lamb liver, otherwise avoid buying that particular dog food.

You should also look for whole grains, and carbohydrate sources like barley, quinoa, sweet potatoes, and wheat. As much as possible avoid processed carbs like brewers rice or wheat mill. Pet food formulators sometimes use one or two food fractions for specific purpose like dried beet pulp or tomato pulp as a fiber source to improve the quality of the dog's stool however, if the entire ingredients list of that particular brand is comprised of nothing but food formulators, then you should stop purchasing it or avoid it in the first place because it might be inexpensive but it is an over-processed food, and it's not good for your dog's health.

Some Important Tips to Remember:

- Don't buy foods that contain artificial colors or sweeteners because dogs, like humans, have sweet receptors but it's not beneficial to your pets overall health. The purpose of sweeteners is to increase the palate ability of the food, but if the food already has the quality, your dog won't need the sugar. It can also contribute to diabetes in the long run.

- Don't buy foods that are preserved with artificial preservatives. However, natural preservatives don't preserve foods for as long as the artificial ones. Make sure to check the dates on the bag. You should know the date of manufacture and the expiration date of the dog food. Each manufacturer sets the date by which the food will still be somehow fresh, wholesome, and full of vitamins and minerals that can degrade overtime.

- Don't purchase any product that is naturally preserved and marked with the code or date that suggest the food is good for more than a year. You should opt to buy a dog food that is recently manufactured.

- You should also look for a product that best matched your dog's need for protein, fat, and calories. Since Min Pins are active and small pets, you may want to buy a high fat, and high protein dog food.

- Make sure to go to your vet and follow their advice regarding the contents of the dog food that is best for your pet's condition.

Types of Commercial Dog Foods

There are three major types of commercial dog foods; these are dry, semi moist, and canned. Dry food contains 6 to 10% moisture, semi moist is 15 to 30% and canned is 75%.

Most canned food has relatively more fat, protein and animal products and lesser carbohydrates than dry and semi-moist food. Pet food labels must list the percentage of protein, fat, fibre, and water in the food. Ask your veterinarian on how to properly read pet food labels so that you can get the most out of the food.

Feeding your dog dry food has two major benefits; the first one is that since it is dry, it won't eat a lot of food which of course would prevent overeating that could lead to obesity; and the second is that it will keep its teeth stronger because of chewing. Be reminded that dry foods should not be the only type of food for your dog's entire diet; you should also feed them fresh ingredients.

Recommended Food Brands for Miniature Pinscher

Feeding your dog a specific diet can make your pet's physique stay stronger, and strengthen its immune system to protect him/her against illnesses especially as they get older. Below are 3 of the most recommended dog food brands for your Min Pins.

Now Fresh Grain – Free Small Breed Recipe

Produced by PetCurean Company, Now Fresh Grain lives up to its name because it is a food brand that contains natural and wholesome ingredients. The PetCurean food brand is family – owned and has a reputation for always delivering good ingredients because of their many trusted suppliers in the food industry. Now Fresh Grain Free Small Breed Recipe dog food is packed with fresh ingredients, and all the essentials needed for your Miniature Pinscher. Its wholesome list of foods is perfect to make your dog well – rounded, and keep its skin and coat healthy.

Here are the high – quality ingredients of the Now Fresh brand that also adheres to the standards mentioned earlier, it also does not contain by – products and artificial ingredients:

- Fresh deboned turkey
- Potatoes
- Egg
- Peas
- Flaxseed
- Apples
- Coconut oil
- Salmon
- Omega-3 and Omega-6 fatty acids

Nutro Small Breed Adult Chicken, Brown Rice & Oatmeal Recipe

Another great dog food company is Nutro. Its line of dog food brands offers a wide range of the finest and freshest ingredients. Nutro also offers variety of product lines with specific formulas for different dog breeds. Some of its product line includes Rotation Revolving Diet, Farm Harvest All Natural Diet, and Ultra dog food lines. The Nutro Small Breed Adult Chicken, Brown Rice & Oatmeal food brand contains two wholesome ingredients; chicken and chicken meal which is a great choice for your Min Pin.

The formulated diet of the Nutro Small Breed food is made up of antioxidants that will boost your dog's immune system, and also meet the high – energy levels of your Min Pin through its protein content. Nutro Small Breed's kibble shape is also beneficial to lessen tartar and plaque build – up which is also very common among Miniature Pinschers and other toy breeds.

Here are the high – quality ingredients of the Nutro Small Breed brand that also adheres to the standards mentioned earlier, it also does not contain by – products and artificial ingredients:

- Whole brown rice
- Whole grain oatmeal
- Chicken fat
- Sunflower Oil
- Targeted levels of Protein

Artemis Fresh Mix Small Breed Adult Formula

Artemis Fresh Mix not just contains natural and high – quality wholesome ingredients, it also follows a holistic approach when it comes to dog nutrition. The company behind the dog food brand also offers a variety of product lines specifically formulated for small, medium and large size dog breeds suitable for puppies and adult dogs. The Artemis Fresh mix is packed with nothing but high – quality animal proteins and other healthy essentials to boost your pet's immune system, and maintain its healthy coat and skin. The product also comes in kibble bite size that your Min Pin will surely enjoy eating.

Here are the high – quality ingredients of the Artemis Fresh Mix brand that also adheres to the standards mentioned earlier, it also does not contain by – products and artificial ingredients:

- Chicken
- Chicken meal
- Turkey
- Fish meal
- Brown rice
- Chicken fat
- Oatmeal
- Salmon oil
- Omega-3 and omega-6 fatty acids

Toxic Foods to Avoid

Some foods are toxic for dogs in general. Make sure that your Min Pin never gets to eat one of the toxic items below, and also ensure that the veterinary checks your dog every now and then. These harmful foods is as important as selecting the right supplements and food items for your dog.

Don't feed your Min Pin with the following:

- Alcohol
- Apple seeds
- Avocado
- Cherry pits
- Chocolates
- Coffee
- Garlic
- Grapes/raisins
- Hops
- Ice Cream
- Macadamia nuts
- Mold

- Mushrooms
- Mustard seeds
- Onions/leeks
- Peach pits
- Potato leaves/stems
- Rhubarb leaves
- Tea
- Tomato leaves/stems
- Walnuts
- Xylitol
- Yeast dough

Tips in Feeding Your Miniature Pinscher

Below are some tips on how to properly feed your dog so that feeding time can be more effective and enjoyable.

- Monitor your dog's weight and adjust intake accordingly. The amount of food required to maintain an ideal body condition will vary depending on age, activity and environment.

- Follow the Feeding Instructions and Recommended Daily Feeding Amounts on the packaging of your pet food. You can also consult your veterinarian regarding the feeding measurement.

- Place the recommended measured amount of food inside the bowl or dish each morning so your dog can eat as he or she pleases throughout the day.

- Use a shallow bowl that your dog can grab food from easily. Try placing the dish in the open to maximize sight lines. It also helps lessen the tension.

- You can find also buy food accessories at your local pet store or even online. Its costs vary depending on the brand of the product

- Always check the feeders after use to make sure your dog is actually eating the recommended daily amount of food.

- For high – energy dogs like the Miniature Pinscher try dividing the daily portion into several bowls and place them in different locations throughout your home.

- Monitor the water intake to make sure your dog is properly hydrated.

Feeding Amount and Frequency

Owning a Min Pin means understanding their feeding requirements. You should be knowledgeable about this because this is very important for their health. At any stage of their lives, they should be given a proper diet to ensure that their body is strong against diseases.

If you are feeding your Min Pins in a wrong way, it may result in some health problems. They may suffer from obesity or other diseases like strained ligaments and joints if you feed them too much. Take note that a puppy burns more calories quickly compared to adults. Therefore, it is very vital to understand the food requirement of your pet depending on his age.

Cheap dog foods contain various harmful ingredients which may affect the health of your pet in a negative way. You have to be aware that various harmful by products and fillers are present in different dog foods and these have almost zero nutrition. It is good if you can feed your dog raw food diet. The amount of food given varies on the age, size, metabolism and the level of the activity of your dog.

It is recommended to free-feed during the first months of your puppy, which means that fresh food should be left out at all times. This is because blood sugar can drop quickly for young puppies, and one cause of this is not eating enough amount of food. For juvenile puppies (around 6 – 12 months old), it is recommended that you feed them three times a day. You may consider buying a treat dispensing toy so that if your dog will not skip a meal if you will be gone during the day.

When it comes to adult Min Pins, they usually eat at least three times a day, although some dogs would be happy with two meals a day. Snacks are reserved for rewarding and training purposes only. It's also recommended that you consult your vet about the proper feeding diet for adult Min Pins because it can vary depending on your pet's condition or health status as they grow older.

There will be changes to the feeding requirements specifically for pregnant, senior, and inactive Min Pins, so it is advised that you first consult with your vet. Younger pups burn more calories compared than older breeds because they have high energy levels, and require food at regular intervals to aid their growth. You may feed your pet three to four times a day at regular intervals, but it is better to consult with your vet because there is no one – size – fits – all diet, feeding amount and frequency will vary.

Chapter Six: Grooming and Training Your Miniature Pinscher

After knowing how to feed your lively Miniature Pinscher a proper diet and nutrition, it's now time to learn how to groom them, and also train them. Aside from being clever dogs, Min Pins are highly trainable breeds; they are naturally curious dogs but needs a very authoritative trainer that can discipline them and keep them grounded. In terms of grooming, you won't have a problem with Min Pins since they are short – coated dogs, although other basic grooming needs like clipping their toes, brushing their teeth, and cleaning their ears are also necessary as part of your dog's hygiene. In this chapter you'll learn some tips on how to train them and maintain their regal poise. This chapter also includes on how to handle their unwanted behaviors.

Training and Dealing with Your Dog's Behavior

Miniature Pinschers are quite self – possess and exuberates a confident and proud finesse. They are one of the most energetic breeds in the toy group category for dogs because of their prancing gait, cleverness, and agility. Min Pin loves to play games, run around the house or backyard, and enjoys vigorous form of activities. Since these dogs have high – levels of energy all day, it's better to put them into good use by teaching them some cool tricks and/or training them around the house so that they will develop proper behavior. If you don't start disciplining them at an early age just like what parents should do to kids, you'll have plenty of headaches in the long run because their intensity can ultimately break lots of household furniture, may develop aggression towards other pets and strangers, and can be a huge problem when you're away. You have to learn how to deal with your dog's behavior as early as possible and do some correction while they're still young so that they will grow up well into their adulthood.

Training Tips for Your Min Pins

This section will give you some tips on how to train your dog to behave properly inside and outside the house, and during shows or competitions (should you decide to enter them in dog competitions).

- Respect Training is the first thing you should teach your dog before you potty train them or teach them how to do some cool tricks. As previously mentioned, you need to be able to establish an authoritative attitude when training Min Pins otherwise you'll have a hard time controlling them.

- Your dog will need leash training. This form of training is about putting him on a leash and then eventually allowing him to go wherever he wants.

- It's also advisable that you enroll your pet in some kind of handling classes; professional trainers will teach your dog to stand beside you when you stop, walk beside you, and teach them how to behave properly.

- If you want to show your dog or join dog competitions, you can also attend conformation training classes. These are to mirror show conditions, which make them an ideal place for show training. These classes will surely help you learn and fine tune all the skills that are required in a show ring.

- When it comes to litter training, what you can do every time your dog pees or poops, is to call out his/her name to cause him to pause, and focus your attention to you.

- As your Min Pin is relieving itself, repeat a chosen word or phrase so that he can associate it with his actions. Some owners use poopy, potty or toilet etc.

- Bring your Min Pin outside with a specific schedule. If you are heading outside to get some exercise, bring him to his bathroom area first. It is highly recommended to have a harness. If you are not used to having one, you may at first think that they are difficult to take on and off, as you go along of course, it will become easier.

- Allow your Min Pin at least five minutes to find the perfect spot within the area, and for his bladder and bowel muscles to relax.

- If your Min Pin is done peeing in the right spot, offer the reward treat right away. Always give praise to them at the same time.

- If your Min Pin misses the 'bathroom area,' don't punish him or her right away. They'll eventually learn in their own time. Make sure to clean the area with an enzyme cleanser.

Here are some of the Min Pin's undesirable traits that you need to deal with while they're still young:

Suspiciousness

Your Min Pins are very suspicious dogs; their natural instinct is to become standoffish but if they're not constantly exposed to people or do not experience unusual sights and sound it can develop into extreme wariness. They will become ferocious or even aggressive if they think that other people or animals are stepping in their "territory." Suspiciousness leads to aggression, your dog may become highly suspicious of everyone, and they are naturally possessive kind of dogs, they will defend what they think is theirs like toys, space or food.

What to do:

To prevent your dog in becoming overly suspicious about everything, it's best that you socialize them and introduce them with other members of the family, strangers, and other animals or household pets if any while they are still puppies. Socialization is very important but it must be supervised. It will also help if you walk your dog everyday around the neighborhood or bring them with you in the city so that they can get used to the noises and the crowds.

Barking and Potential Aggression

You won't have a problem with excessive barking and potential aggression if you have done some respect training to your dog or if you have properly socialize them early on. Excessive barking is caused by suspiciousness; most Min Pins are too quick to respond to various sounds or alarms, this should be regulated though otherwise your dog will bark whenever they feel like it which will produce inconvenience to you or your neighbor especially if you're staying in an apartment. Being cautious is different from being suspicious. You have to teach them to actively respond or become aggressive at things that is really suspicious or things that could pose a threat to your household.

What to do:

Most Min Pins are naturally dominant animals even to large dog breeds. As previously mentioned, they like to launch themselves towards bigger dogs to prove that they are also powerful despite their small size. They will also prey on small pets, which is why it is not advised to keep smaller animals like guinea pigs, rabbits or birds around the house. What you can do aside from socializing them and training them to follow you is to avoid making them mingle with other dominant, larger breed of dogs or leaving small pets around the house. Yes, you can introduce other dogs or smaller animals to them but make sure that you supervise them when you do so, and if you think that they are becoming aggressive because of their natural instinct, it's probably best to avoid exposing them constantly to such animals so that this destructive behavior will not be triggered and repeated.

Housebreaking Tips

A Min Pin that is not fully housebroken should never be free in either a room or the house especially if he is not well - supervised because they can trash your place real quick even if they are small in size. You should always reward your dog/s with treats if you want them to be more motivated to focus in behaving properly, learn more during training, and look forward to the next training lesson.

Guidelines in Grooming Your Miniature Pinscher

As mentioned in previous chapters, Miniature Pinschers are low maintenance when it comes to grooming. Of course, if grooming is not performed properly or on a regular basis, things can go out of control. The skin may dry out, tear stains might become excessive, and your dog's paws and nose might peel. In short, it can become a disaster. Min Pins' coats are very short, and they also don't shed compare to other dogs but you still need to check their grooming status every once in a while.

- Make sure to clip your Min Pin's toenails with dog toenail clippers once every six or eight weeks. It will keep your dog's paws clean and healthy and will prevent him from scratching upon jumping up. Be sure not to cut their nails too close as this may hurt them

- You have to thoroughly brush your Min Pin's teeth on a regular basis so that they won't get dental cavities. You have to use special toothpaste that contains enzymes to inhibit bacterial growth in the mouth.

- Min Pin's bright and almond shape eyes can potentially have an eye discharge that may cause an infection due to bacteria. Be sure to clean or remove any unwanted discharge from your dog's eyes.

- Your Min Pin does not need to be shaved down during hot weather. You can do a bit of trimming just to keep things clean and neat, you can do that every 2 to 3 months or as needed.

Chapter Seven: Showing Your Miniature Pinscher

The Miniature Pinschers are elegant dogs with a spirited presence. The best part is that even though they are not officially eligible for dog shows since they are a toy breed, you can still sign up your dog for different training and showing competitions for small and local dog organizations. Your Min Pin has the potential to be so much more than just a house pet, but before you show your pet, you have to make sure that he/she meets the requirements for the breed standard and also learn some basic tips on how to prepare yourself and your pet. In this chapter you will learn more about the specific standard for the Min Pin breed, learn some show training tips, and also some guidelines on the things you need to keep in mind so you and your pet can enjoy the competition.

American Kennel Club Miniature Pinscher Breed Standard

General

- The body should be sturdy, short – coupled, well – balanced and compact.
- It must also be smooth - coated
- Must be well – groomed, alert, vigorous and have a proud projection.
- Must appear self – possessed, spirited, and fearless
- Should be physically, and temperamentally well – balanced and/or trained.

Head

- Must be proportionate to the body
- The head should not be too prominent. It must be tapering and narrow with a well – fitted foreface that balances with the skull.

- There should be no indication of coarseness
- The skull should appear flat and tapering towards the muzzle.

Muzzle

- Must not be strong rather than fine and delicate
- Should be proportionate to the head
- Must be parallel to the top of the skull

Ears

- Should be high and erect from its base to the tip
- It could be cropped or uncropped

Eyes

- Should be slightly oval in shape
- Must be clear, bright, and have a darkish black eye color including its eye rims (except for chocolate colored Min Pins – the eye rims should be self – colored).

Nose, Bite, Lips

- The nose must be black in color (except for chocolate colored Min Pins – the nose should be self – colored).
- The lips as well as the cheeks should be taut and adherent to each other
- Its teeth should have a scissors bite

Body

- The neck should be proportionate to the head and body. It must be slight arched and blending into the shoulders.
- The neck must also be gracefully curved, muscular, and free from dewlap or throatiness.
- Its topline or back should be sloping toward the rear side whenever he/she is standing and gaiting.
- The whole body must be slightly wedge in shape and muscular.
- Forechest should be well – develop, and the ribs should be well – sprung.
- The belly or tummy should be slightly tucked to show structural form
- Must have short and strong loins

Forequarters

- The shoulders should be sloping with a moderate angulation to permit a hackney – like action
- The elbows should be closed to the body
- The legs must have strong bone development and healthy joints
- Pasterns must be strong and perpendicular
- There should be no dewclaws
- The forefeet must have small and catlike toes that are well – arched and knitted with deep pads; its nails should be thick and blunt

Hindquarters

- Must have muscular hindquarters that are set wide enough to have a proportionate body.
- The legs should be straight and parallel when viewed from the rear side
- Thighs must be muscular
- Stifles should be well – defined, the hocks should also be set wide enough
- There should be no dewclaws
- The forefeet must have small and catlike toes that are well – arched and knitted with deep pads; its nails should be thick and blunt

Tail

- Should be high and erect
- Must be docked and the size should be proportionate to the dog's body.

Coat

- Must be smooth and short
- Mist be straight, hard and lustrous
- Should uniformly cover the entire body.

Coat Color

- Should be solid clear red or stag red (with black hairs intermingling)
- Black with well – defined rust – red marking on the cheeks, lips, jaw, throat, and should be twin spot in the eyes and chest.
- The Chocolate with rusty red markings should be covered in the same spots as specified for black colored Min Pins

Gait

- The forelegs and back legs should be parallel with feet neither in nor out

- Must have a hackney – like action (it is a high – stepping, free and easy gait wherein the front leg moves straight forward and in front of the body; the foot bends at the wrist similar to how horses walk).
- The dog should drive smoothly from the rear
- The head and tail should be held high while walking

Disqualification

- If the dog is under 10 inches or over 12 ½ inches in height
- Any color other than the three major colors listed above
- White spot on any part of the dog's body that exceeds ½ inches.
- Thumb mark that has a patch of black hair

Guidelines before Presenting Your Miniature Pinscher

Make sure that you familiarized yourself with the rules and regulations for a particular show in which you plan to enter your dog; showing your dog can be a wonderful experience but it can also be quite challenging. To ensure that your dog does well in the show, he/she needs to be a strong example of the breed standard. There are also some general things you can do to prepare for a dog show like your dog's pedigree and registration papers, veterinary records and proof of vaccinations, litter pan and dog litter, food treats or food/water bowls, blanket or bed for the cage, necessary grooming equipment like nail clippers, brush etc. Don't also forget the confirmation slip you received to prove that your dog is registered and qualified.

Here are some guidelines in preparing your dog for show:

- Make sure your dog is properly pedigreed according to the regulations of the show – you may need to present your dog's papers/ license as proof so make sure to have them ready.

- Make sure to fill out the registration form correctly, providing all of the necessary details, and turn it in on time.

- Prepare to pay a registration fee as well or a competition fee if any.

- Clip your dog's claws before the show.

- Make sure that your dog is registered with the organization running the show.

- Make sure to enter your dog in the proper age bracket or category because some organizations do not allow very young puppies while other has some restrictions.

- Find out what is provided by the show and what you need to bring for yourself – some competitions provide an exhibition cage but you will need to bring some things.

- Be prepared to spend all day at the show and bring with you everything you and your dog may need to make it through the day.

- Pay close attention to all of the information the show gives you with your registration, some shows provide a list of recommended materials to bring either through their website or it may be directly sent to your email.

- You can go far beyond basic commands in training a Min Pin if you are committed; these dogs are very well known for their highly trainable traits.

- You need to understand that training for a show requires a lot of hard work because the lessons are much complicated than basic housebreaking training.

- You should learn how to properly groom your dog for a show. You can get it from a professional book, from a video or from a groomer itself. You should make grooming an enjoyable experience just like dog training. It will surely help your pet get used to grooming because this will help him become more accustomed to being handled.

- Practice posing or stacking your dog as soon as he is comfortable with the grooming table. First, have him stay in his position for a few seconds. And then increase the time you make him stay on the table. Be sure to give him a lot of rewards for standing poised for a long period of time.

Before deciding to enter your Min Pin/s in a dog show, you should first attend a few shows so you can have an idea. The more you and your dog are prepared for a show, the more your training will pay off.

Chapter Eight: Breeding Your Miniature Pinscher

Do you want to try your hands in breeding more of this cute and energetic bunch? Or perhaps become a reputable breeder? In this chapter you'll be provided with information about breeding basics of Min Pins, their mating process, pregnancy FAQs, and some guidelines on how to raise puppies so you'll have an idea if you want to become a legit breeder. Aside from knowing the basics though, you also have to consider your financial capacity, attention, and time. This is because breeding involves lots of expenses, and puppies need to be taken care of, maintained, and supervise. To know more about breeding your dog, turn the page now!

Breeding Basics

The first rule that to you have to understand and follow is that breeding is best left to professional breeders. But of course, it is also essential that you know the basics of breeding a dog. A lot of things are involved, and it is important that you know your responsibilities and all the things that you need to observe to ensure that the breeding will produce healthy Min Pin puppies.

There is somewhat a high level of loss in puppies. This is caused by different kinds of reasons, and can also happen in any breed not only among Min Pins, but this happens more often in toy breeds. Lots of breeders today use lab tests to measure progesterone and vaginal cytology to determine when ovulation occurs. The cycle is usually twenty days. What may be normal for one dog may differ from another.

During the first day of heating, you might notice some changes like the swelling of your dog's vulva because of the reddish discharge coming out; you'll also notice that she is constantly licking its rear. After about five days, the main physical change you'll notice is the continuous swelling of its vulva and a blood discharge like a menstruation in female humans. After about ten days, the color of your dog's vulva lightens up a bit, and the vulva will have a moist or soft appearance. In about fourteen days, your dog's vulva will become clear, and its edges will begin to harden up. Swelling and discharge will be almost gone as well. This will continue until the 21st day, by then it means that your female dog or bitch is ready for mating.

Signs that Your Female Dog is ready for Mating

When a female dog or what they termed it as the 'bitch' is in heat, there are a few signs that can point towards her beginning this process such as being nervous, easily distracted, some signs of increasing appetite, and urinating more than usual. Your female dog's personality may also alter due to the abrupt change in her hormones. Male dogs in general are ready to breed from the age of 18 months to 4/5 years old.

Pregnancy FAQs

How can I increase my dog's chances for successful mating/breeding?

To increase your chances of a successful breeding, you need to keep track of your Min Pin's estrus cycle. Once your female reaches the point of ovulation, you can introduce her to the male dog and let nature take its course. Breeding behavior varies slightly from one breed to another, but you can expect the male dog to mount the female from behind after her heat cycle. If the breeding is successful, conception will occur and the gestation period will begin.

How long is the gestation period for my pregnant dog?

Min Pins have a gestation period lasting about 59 - 63 days (or about 8 to 9 weeks). The gestation period is the period of time following conception during which the puppies develop in the mother's uterus.

What is the average litter size for Min Pins?

The average litter size for the Min Pin breed is between 2 to 4 puppies, some Min Pins can reach a maximum of 6 or more newborns. Keep in mind that new mothers will often have smaller litters – the next few litters will generally be larger before the litter size starts to taper off again.

How do I feed my pregnant dog?

You need to take special care to make sure your bitch is properly nourished. You do not need to make changes to your dog's diet until the fourth or fifth week of pregnancy.

At that point you should slightly increase her daily rations in an amount proportionate to her weight gain. It is generally best to offer your dog free feeding because she will know how much she needs to eat. Make sure your dog's diet is high in protein as well as calories, calcium, and fat to support the development of her puppies.

How do I know if my dog is ready to give birth?

Once your Min Pins starts going into labor, you can expect her to show some obvious signs of discomfort. Your dog might start pacing restlessly, panting, and switching positions. The early stages of labor can often last for several hours and contractions may occur as often as 10 minutes apart. If your pet has contractions for more than 2 hours without any of the puppies being born, contact your veterinarian immediately. Once your dog starts giving birth, the puppies will arrive about every thirty minutes following ten to thirty minutes of straining.

Another sign is if your dog's body temperature drops. Prior to labor, your dog's body temperature may drop as low as 98°F (36.6°C); the normal dog temperature is 100°F to 102°F (37.7°C to 38.8°C). Once its temperature drops, you can expect contractions to begin within 24 hours or so – if it gets any lower, contact your veterinarian.

Where should I put the box for whelping?

Whelping is the time to set up a whelping box where your female dog can comfortably give birth to her puppies. Place the box in a quiet, dim area and line it with newspapers and old towels for comfort. The closer it gets to giving birth, the more time your dog will spend in the whelping box because she is also preparing it for her litter.

Why is Colostrum important for newborn puppies?

Colostrum is the first milk produced from the puppy's mother. It contains a variety of nutrients as well as antibodies to protect the pups until their own immune systems develop.

Raising Puppies

After each puppy is born, dogs will lick its puppy clean; it may even eat the umbilical cord since it is animal instinct. This also helps to stimulate the puppy to start breathing on his own. Once all of the puppies have been born, the mother will expel the rest of the placenta then let the puppies start nursing. It is essential that the puppies begin nursing within one hour of being born because this is when they will receive the colostrum from the mother.

Min Pin puppies are relatively small in size since it is a toy breed. As the puppies grow, they will start to become increasingly active and they will grow very quickly as long as they are properly fed by their mother or by you. The puppies should be six weeks old before you wean them, you can do this by offering them small amounts of puppy food soaked in water or broth. The puppies might sample small bits of solid food even while they are still nursing and the mother will general wean the puppies by the eight week, with or without your help. If you plan to sell the puppies, be sure not to send them home unless they are fully weaned at least 8 weeks old. You should also take steps to start socializing the puppies from an early age to make sure they turn into well - adjusted adults.

Chapter Nine: Common Diseases and Health Requirements

In this chapter you will be provided with some of the most common health problems affecting Min Pins. If you are aware of the possible diseases and disorders that may cause trouble for your pet, it can be potentially lifesaving and also will prevent you from touching your savings! As what they always say, prevention is better than cure. You as the potential dog keeper should also learn how to strengthen your dog's resistance to common illnesses by giving them the necessary vaccinations and through having regular checkup with their vets.

Common Health Problems

In this section, you will learn about the diseases that may affect and threaten your Min Pin. Learning these diseases as well as its remedies is vital for you and your dog so that you could prevent it from happening or even help with its treatment in case they caught one.

Minor Problems:

Kennel Cough

Kennel cough is a type of bronchitis, and it is easily transmitted between dogs. It usually affects the dogs breathing and voice box; most of the time it presents itself as a harsh cough, sneezing or even vomiting. Kennel cough can progress to pneumonia if left untreated, so better take care of it as soon as possible. Vaccines or shots are available to prevent your dog from easily getting affected with Kennel Cough from other dogs. If your Min Pin is constantly in contact with other dogs, doctors suggest that you give them a vaccination twice a year or every 6 months, so that your dog will be immune for the whole year.

Lyme Disease

The Lyme disease is caused by ticks and parasites that attach themselves to your dog. These parasites feed on the host's blood, and transmit diseases like Lyme disease. The common symptoms of Lyme disease are fever, limping or other neurological disease which can kill your dog (if left untreated) depending on where it is located in the body. If you found out that your dog has ticks, you can treat it with topical treatment/s that treats fleas and ticks. You should consult your vet on which brand is best for your pet.

Arthritis

Arthritis is very common among toy breeds. Your Min Pin can develop arthritis as they grow older or as they age. It actually increases its effect, if a dog is born with hip dysplasia (which is also very common in small dog breeds). The good news is that, it is a manageable condition, and it's best to get an early diagnosis from your vet. If you want to prevent your Min Pin in suffering from arthritis, the best you can do is to maintain its diet, and keep him/her as lean as possible. Medications can aid your dog if ever he/she develops arthritis but doctors suggest that good exercise and proper diet is essential.

Hip Dysplasia

Hip dysplasia is a very common musculoskeletal problem among small breed of dogs like the Min Pins. In a normal hip, the part of the thigh bone sits snugly within the groove of the hip joint and it rotates freely within the grove as the dog moves. Hip dysplasia occurs when the femoral head becomes separated from the hip joint – this is called subluxation. This could occur as a result of abnormal joint structure or laxity in the muscles and ligaments supporting the joint. This condition can present in pups as young as five months of age or in senior dogs.

Major Problems:

Heart Disease

Just like humans, dogs are also at risk of developing abnormal enlargements in their hearts, though that doesn't mean that your pet will not live a normal life. Aging could be a factor of heart diseases in dogs but other issues like heartworms, improper diet and the likes can also lead to having major heart problems. Some of the symptoms include being out of breath, having problems in a hot condition/weather, not as active as before, hypertension, obesity, other illnesses resulting to complications etc. If you think that your dog is showing any signs of slowing down, you might want to consult with your vet so that your dog will have proper assessment and treatment.

Cancer

Cancer is affecting more dogs than ever especially young puppies. Dogs in the toy group like older or adult Min Pins or pooches are the most affected among other breeds. Symptoms include lumps, swelling, lesions or sudden changes in your dog's behavior. What you can do to prevent the cancer from spreading and to hopefully save your dog's life is to have him/her regularly checked by the vet so that they can diagnose the disease as soon as possible and give proper treatment. Treatments like chemotherapy and medicinal options are the usual solutions for cancers in dogs, just like in humans and other household pets.

Obesity

Your Min Pin's health can be negatively affected if he/she is overweight. Obesity is not just common among small dog breeds, it affects other medium to large size breeds as well, and even other pets like cats. You should keep your pets as healthy, lean, and in shape as much as possible to help avoid complications like diabetes, heart problems, and joint disease. It's highly recommended that you work with your vet to create an exercise plan that fits your Min Pin's lifestyle. Active dogs like pinschers, needs different amount of sustenance but it's also important not to restrict the amount of food that you're giving to your dog otherwise they may become malnourished.

Dental Disease

Dental disease affects dogs around two years old and above. Gum disease is a very common and potentially serious health problem that your Min Pin can face. If you notice that your dog has a stinky breath, it only means that the disease has already progress further. It will eventually lead to tartar buildup; tartar is a bacteria, and as it accumulates it can eventually enter the body through the gums. If you don't give enough attention, dental disease can lead to various heart problems, diabetes, kidney disease, and other serious or potentially fatal problems. The best way to prevent gum diseases is to simply brush their teeth at least once a day or every other day. You can consult your vet about the specific kind of dog toothpaste you can purchase for your Min Pin, because fluorine (contained in human toothpaste) is toxic for your pet.

Vaccinations for Puppies and Adult Dogs

Puppies are born with a vulnerable immune system, which makes them unable to protect themselves against diseases. This is the reason why they need colostrum that contains antibodies that will protect the pups, but the antibodies provided through the colostrum are only limited. Around 45 days, when the puppy's immune systems are mature enough, the pup's vaccination can begin. All dogs, including Min Pins need shots or vaccinations to help prevent diseases and make their body's immune system stronger. Your vet will be making a recommendation, but normally, your pet will get these general vaccines similar to other dog breed.

There are two types of vaccines; essential, and optional. Essential vaccines protects the puppies from major diseases, these are the basic vaccines that your dog needs. It can also be found around the world. Optional vaccines, on the other hand, are only found or are necessary in certain locations or regions, which is why it may not be always administer. Also keep in mind that a vaccine that is optional in one country maybe mandatory in another country or region.

Essential Vaccines include the following:

- Canine distemper
- Infectious hepatitis
- Parvovirus
- Canine Rabies

Optional Vaccines include the following:

- Leptospirosis
- Coronavirus
- Canine Parainfluenza
- Lyme disease
- Kennel Cough (caused by Bortadella)

Vaccination Schedule

It's important to get your Min Pin a shot even if it seems that he is too small to have one because this is vital to their health. Puppies first get their shots as soon as they leave their moms; vets usually recommend starting vaccines when puppies are already eight to nine weeks old, though sometimes some pups already get a vaccine shot as early as 6 weeks old.

When puppies get boosters, they get a natural immunity from their moms but it interferes with the shots that you gave to them. The best thing to do is give your puppy a series of shots to make sure he's covered when he needs it. Min Pins should be getting boosters every two to four weeks until he's 16 weeks old. As soon as he is finished with puppy shots, give your dog a booster shots once every three years but if your vet recommends annual boosters, follow it and go with that schedule.

Each vet can recommend a different schedule depending on the dog's situation. Aside from a rabies shot, other vaccines include a polyvalent vaccine, and leptospirosis. Polyvalent vaccine contains the adenovirus that protects your dog from kennel cough, and infectious hepatitis. It also protects against distemper and parvovirus. Below are the recommended vaccine schedules for your Min Pin. Leptospirosis vaccine will protect your dog against toxic diseases caused by a rat's urine that can enter your dog's bloodstream through a wound from a contaminated water source. Annual revaccinations for adult dogs include Polyvalent, Leptospirosis, and Canine Rabies.

Below are the suggested schedule of vaccines for puppies and dogs:

- Week 8: Multipurpose
- Week 12: Polyvalent and Leptospirosis
- Week 16: Polyvalent and Leptospirosis
- Week 24: Rabies

First Aid Treatments

Medical emergencies may happen to your dog from time to time. Your dog may require immediate veterinary care, but first aid methods may help in stabilizing your pet for transportation or while you are waiting for the medic to arrive. Here are some first aid treatment tips for you:

- If the dog is suffering from bleeding because of trauma, try to elevate and apply pressure to the wound.

- If your pet is choking, place your fingers inside his mouth and see if you can remove the blockage. If you cannot remove the foreign object, perform a modified Heimlich maneuver by giving a sharp rap to his chest which will dislodge the object.

- Perform a CPR if your dog became unconscious. You can do this by placing him on his side and perform an artificial respiration by extending his neck and head, holding his jaws closed and by blowing into his nostrils once every 3 seconds.

- You can also incorporate a cardiac massage, while having artificial respiration if your dog is still not breathing after blowing his nostrils. Just do a three quick, firm chest compression for every respiration until your dog can breathe normally already.

- If you think your dog has ingested toxic food or substance, call your vet immediately or the ASPCA Animal Poison Control Center's 24-hour hotline at (888) 426 – 4435.Follow the vet's suggested recommendation, because they will first consider the age and health of your dog and what and how he ate a certain poisonous food. You can also try to let your pet drink a milk of magnesia to aid for the meantime.

- It's also recommended that you always have with you an emergency bag at all times containing supplies like food, water, medications/medical history (if any), proof of recent vaccinations, proof of ownership, leashes, pet carrier, first aid kit (gauze, hydrogen peroxide, milk of magnesia (for poisoning conditions).

Chapter Ten: Care Sheet and Summary

Always keep in mind that being a dog keeper goes beyond in just taking care of their basic needs, and keeping them for keeping's sake. You should be able to go the extra mile if you decide to be the care taker of this wonderful and energetic pet. Make sure to meet its habitat needs, physical needs as well as its mental and emotional demands to ensure that he/she will live happily with your or your family, and be a great companion for many years. In this chapter, we will give you a quick summary of the major points you need to remember that was discussed in this book. A quick glance can be of help if you are in a hurry or if you simply wanted to review something important.

Biological Information

Taxonomy: Kingdom Animalia, Phylum Chordata, Class Mammalia, Order Carnivora, Family Canidae, Genus Canis, Species Canis lupus.

Country of Origin: Germany

Breed Size: small – size breed

Body Type and Appearance: Has a small, compact, and well – balanced body with proportionate legs, bright eyes, cropped ears, docked tail and tapering head.

Weight: average of 8 – 10 pounds

Coat Length: short and smooth coat

Coat Texture: smooth, soft, well - groomed

Color: Red, Black & Rust, and Chocolate & Rust colors

Other Names: Min Pins, Mini Pin

Miniature Pinscher as Pets

Temperament: energetic, fearless, friendly, sociable, and affectionate

Other pets: friendly with other pets in general, but if not properly introduce may result to potential aggression

Major Pro: has a loyal, fearless, and fun personality, short – coated which means that you won't have any problem in terms of grooming them, a lap dog and a trainable breed.

Major Con: Needs lots of exercise and a space to play with, excessive barking and housebreaking difficulties; may need an authoritative trainer.

Legal Requirements and Dog Licensing:

U.S. and U.K.: There are no federal requirements for licensing dogs but it is regulated at the state level. However, you will need to get a special permit if you plan to travel with your dog into or out of the country. Dogs may also be subjected to quarantine.

Other countries: Bring proper documents such as your state permit for your dog, rabies or vaccinations certificate, and current health condition, and other requirements as deemed necessary.

Purchasing and Selecting a Healthy Breed

Where to Purchase: Private/Reputable Breeders, Backyard Breeders, Pet Stores (although it is not recommended)

Characteristics of a Reputable Breeder: Expect a reputable breeder to ask you questions about yourself as well. Another sign is that if the breeders joins its dogs for showing competitions because it means that he/she likes to adheres to the dog's breed standard

Characteristics of a Healthy Breed: Examine the dogs' or body thoroughly for any signs of illness and potential injuries. Also see to it that the pup is behaving properly.

Habitat Requirements for Miniature Pinscher: Provide play pen, comfortable bedding, toys and other essential accessories. Make sure that the cage or play pen is placed in a nice location.

Housing Temperature: should still be at a normal range, not too hot and not too cold.

Nutrition and Food

- Feed your Min Pins a healthy home prepared, and well – formulated diet that contains fresh ingredients as well as canned, frozen, dehydrated and/or kibble foods.

Recommended Brands of Miniature Pinscher Foods: Now Fresh Grain – Free Small Breed Recipe, Nutro Small Breed Adult Chicken, Brown Rice & Oatmeal Recipe, Artemis Fresh Mix Small Breed Adult Formula

How to Feed Your Dog: For high – energy dogs like the Miniature Pinscher try dividing the daily portion into several bowls and place them in different locations throughout your home.

Feeding Amount/Frequency: For juvenile puppies (around 6 – 12 months old). When it comes to adult Min Pins, they usually eat at least three times a day, although some dogs would be happy with two meals a day. There will be changes to the feeding requirements specifically for pregnant, senior, and inactive Min Pins, so it is advised that you first consult with your vet. (See Chapter 5 for further info)

Grooming and Training Your Miniature Pinscher

How to Brush Your Dog's Teeth: Ideally you should be brushing your dog's teeth every day or every other day to avoid dental or gum diseases

How to Trim Your Dog's Nails: Make sure to clip your Min Pin's toenails with dog toenail clippers once every six or eight weeks.

Trimming Your Dog's Coat: You can do a bit of trimming just to keep things clean and neat, you can do that every 2 to 3 months or as needed.

Showing Your Miniature Pinscher

- The body should be sturdy, short – coupled, well – balanced and compact.

- It must also be smooth - coated

- Must be well – groomed, alert, vigorous and have a proud projection.

- Must appear self – possessed, spirited, and fearless

- Should be physically, and temperamentally well – balanced and/or trained.

(See Breed Standard in Chapter 7 for complete list)

Breeding Your Miniature Pinscher

Gestation Period: 59 - 63 days (or about 8 to 9 weeks).

Litter Size: Min Pins typically give birth to 2 - 4 kittens on average and up to a maximum of 6 puppies or more.

Maturity: Min Pins become mature around 6 to 9 months of age.

Common Diseases and Health Requirements

- **Minor Diseases:**
- Kennel Cough
- Lyme disease
- Arthritis
- Hip Dysplasia

- **Major Diseases:**
- Heart Disease
- Cancer
- Dental Disease

Recommended Vaccinations:

- Canine distemper
- Infectious hepatitis
- Parvovirus
- Canine Rabies
- Leptospirosis
- Coronavirus
- Canine Parainfluenza
- Lyme disease
- Kennel Cough (caused by Bortadella)

Glossary of Dog Terms

AKC – abbreviation for American Kennel Club; it is the biggest dog registry organization in America

Almond Eye – Refers to an elongated eye shape. It appears as an oblong shape and not roundish or circular

Apple Head – A skull that has a round-shaped

Balance – It is a jargon show term which refers to the dog's movement when standing and/or walking that also projects a harmonious image.

Beard – Refers to the long, and/or thick hair in the underjaw of dogs

Best in Show – A show term that refers to a form of recognition; it is given to the undefeated dog during competitions.

Bitch – A female dog

Bite – It is when the upper and lower teeth of the dog touches as it closes its jaws; it can either be a level bite, undershot bite, scissors, and overshot bite.

Blaze – It is a white stripe that can be found in the center of the face between the dog's eyes

Board – To house, feed, and care for a dog for a fee

Breed – a race of dogs that have a common gene pool or a dog's characterization based on its appearance, function or personality.

Breed Standard – It is a document that describes the official standard from a certain dog registry or organization that specifies the appearance, movement and the dog's behavior.

Buff – It is a white to gold coloring

Clip – A term that refers in cutting the coat for some breeds

Coat – Has two types; an outer coat and an undercoat (or double coat). It refers to the skin or fur of the dog breed

Condition – The condition of a dog in terms of its coat, body appearance, temperament, and overall behavior.

Crate – Similar to a cage or kennel; use to transport dogs and serves as a shelter

Crossbreed (Hybrid) – A dog having a sire and the offspring of two different dog breeds. These types of dog cannot be officially registered in some dog registry because it is not purebred.

Dam (bitch) – The female parent of a dog

Drop Ear – It refers to the kind of ear that folds over and hangs down. It is neither prick nor erect

Dock Tail – A shorten form of tail in dogs. Sometimes owners also surgically cut their dog's tail, making it shorter or docked.

Fancier – A person interested in a particular dog breed.

Feathering – It is the long hair in the dog's tail, legs, body or ears

Groom – Refers to the act of brushing, trimming, or combing the dog's fur or skin making the coat neat in appearance

Heel – A command to dogs which means to stay close by the owner's side

Hip Dysplasia – A condition characterized by the abnormal formation of the hip joint

Inbreeding – The breeding of two closely related dogs of one breed

Kennel – Refers to the dog's enclosure

Litter – Refers to the group of puppies born at the same time

Markings – A pattern or flashes of color on a dog's coat

Mask – The darkish part on the dog's foreface

Mate – The act of sexing a male dog and a female dog to produce puppies

Neuter – To castrate a male dog or spay a female dog or remove their reproductive system to avoid unwanted pregnancies.

Pads – The thick skin at the bottom of a dog's foot or paw.

Parti-Color – A coloration of a dog's coat consisting of two or more definite, well-broken colors; one of the colors must be white

Pedigree – It refers to the record of a dog's genealogy that goes back to its parents, grandparents, and ancestors.

Pied – Refers to a coloration consisting of white patches and another color

Prick Ear – Ear that is carried erect, usually pointed at the tip of the ear

Puppy – A dog under 12 months of age; a newborn dog

Purebred – A dog that came from the same pedigree or breed group

Saddle – Colored markings in the shape of a saddle over the back; colors may vary

Shedding – The natural process whereby old hair falls off the dog's body as it is replaced by new hair growth.

Sire – The dog's father or male parent

Smooth Coat – close – lying short hairs on the dog's skin

Spay – The surgical procedure to remove the reproductive system of a female dog making her incapable of breeding

Trim – To pluck or clip a dog's hair

Undercoat – Located under the longer outer coat; usually soft and silky.

Wean – Refers to a process in which puppies transition from drinking colostrum from their mom's milk to eating dog foods.

Whelping – Happens during the labor of a pregnant bitch

Index

C

D

H

I

J

K

L

M

N

O

S

T

U

V

W

Photo Credits

Page 1 Photo by user syesko via Pixabay.com, https://pixabay.com/en/min-pin-miniature-small-pin-breed-2127876/

Page 5 Photo by user Ernst Moeksis via Flickr.com, https://www.flickr.com/photos/16961193@N06/2497103953/

Page 12 Photo by user Malenga via Flickr.com, https://www.flickr.com/photos/malenga/507963538/

Page 24 Photo by user Alberta Armstrong via Wikimedia Commons, https://commons.wikimedia.org/wiki/File:Min_pin_ear_detail.jpg

Page 37 Photo by user Slayer63b via Wikimedia Commons, https://commons.wikimedia.org/wiki/File:A_four_month_old_Min_Pin_(Tiara)_with_white_markings_on_her_chest.JPG

Page 46 Photo by user glenn_e_wilson via Wikimedia Commons, https://commons.wikimedia.org/wiki/File:Miniature_Pinscher_Flickr.jpg

Page 60 Photo by user troy_williams via Flickr.com, https://www.flickr.com/photos/troy_williams/15316753503/

Page 70 Photo by user Ly.H. via Flickr.com, https://www.flickr.com/photos/lylo0u/4743485648/

References

"10 Telling Signs That the Breeder You're Buying from Is Bad News" – AngusPost.com
http://anguspost.com/10-telling-signs-that-the-breeder/

"Breeding - What to Expect After Mating" – Vetwest.com
https://www.vetwest.com.au/pet-library/breeding-what-to-expect-after-mating

"How to Recognize a Bad Dog Breeder" – Dummies.com
http://www.dummies.com/pets/dogs/how-to-recognize-a-bad-dog-breeder/

"Miniature Pinscher" Dogtime.com
http://dogtime.com/dog-breeds/miniature-pinscher#/slide/1

"Miniature Pinscher" American Kennel Club
http://www.akc.org/dog-breeds/miniature-pinscher/

"Miniature Pinscher" Vetstreet.com
http://www.vetstreet.com/dogs/miniature-pinscher

"Miniature Pinscher" Wikipedia.com
https://en.wikipedia.org/wiki/Miniature_Pinscher

"Miniature Pinscher (Min Pin)" Petbreeds.com
http://dogs.petbreeds.com/l/103/Miniature-Pinscher-Min-Pin

"Miniature Pinscher at a Glance" Hillspet.com
http://www.hillspet.com/en/us/dog-breeds/miniature-pinscher

"Miniature Pinscher: Breed And Health Information" - Petcarex.Com
https://www.petcarerx.com/article/miniature-pinscher-breed-and-health-information/349

"Miniature Pinscher (Min Pin) Health Care & Feeding" – Your Pure Bred Puppy
http://www.yourpurebredpuppy.com/health/miniaturepinschers.html

"Miniature Pinscher - Temperament & Personality" Petwave.com
http://www.petwave.com/Dogs/Breeds/Miniature-Pinscher/Personality.aspx

"Signs of a Bad Breeder or a Backyard Breeder" – The Spruce
https://www.thespruce.com/signs-of-a-bad-breeder-1117328

"Signs Your Dog Is Pregnant" - Pethelpful.com
https://pethelpful.com/dogs/Signs-your-dog-is-pregnant

"The Best Dog Foods for Miniature Pinschers" - Dog Food Insider

https://www.dogfoodinsider.com/best-dog-foods-miniature-pinschers/

Feeding Baby
Cynthia Cherry
978-1941070000

Axolotl
Lolly Brown
978-0989658430

Dysautonomia, POTS
Syndrome
Frederick Earlstein
978-0989658485

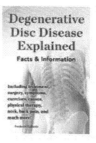

Degenerative Disc
Disease Explained
Frederick Earlstein
978-0989658485

Sinusitis, Hay Fever,
Allergic Rhinitis Explained
Frederick Earlstein
978-1941070024

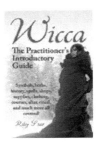

Wicca
Riley Star
978-1941070130

Zombie Apocalypse
Rex Cutty
978-1941070154

Capybara
Lolly Brown
978-1941070062

Eels As Pets
Lolly Brown
978-1941070167

Scabies and Lice Explained
Frederick Earlstein
978-1941070017

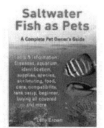

Saltwater Fish As Pets
Lolly Brown
978-0989658461

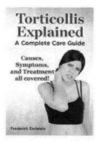

Torticollis Explained
Frederick Earlstein
978-1941070055

Kennel Cough
Lolly Brown
978-0989658409

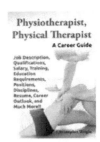

Physiotherapist, Physical
Therapist
Christopher Wright
978-0989658492

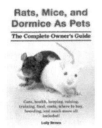

Rats, Mice, and Dormice
As Pets
Lolly Brown
978-1941070079

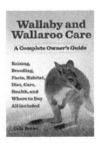

Wallaby and Wallaroo Care
Lolly Brown
978-1941070031

Bodybuilding Supplements
Explained
Jon Shelton
978-1941070239

Demonology
Riley Star
978-19401070314

Pigeon Racing
Lolly Brown
978-1941070307

Dwarf Hamster
Lolly Brown
978-1941070390

Cryptozoology
Rex Cutty
978-1941070406

Eye Strain
Frederick Earlstein
978-1941070369

Inez The Miniature Elephant
Asher Ray
978-1941070353

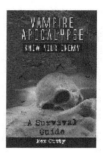

Vampire Apocalypse
Rex Cutty
978-1941070321

Printed in Great Britain
by Amazon